# HOW TO GET RICH

## ON THE

# OREGON TRAIL

## MY ADVENTURES AMONG COWS, CROOKS & HEROES ON THE ROAD TO FAME AND FORTUNE

*If the family makes the journey west, you will need a place to record your experiences. Do not forget your grandfather when you make your first fortune as a writer.*

*S. R.*

WRITING JOURNAL OF:

### Master William Reed

PORTLAND, OREGON
1852

GIFT OF MR. SILAS REED

NATIONAL GEOGRAPHIC

WASHINGTON, D.C.

March 23, 2004

To the editors of National Geographic:

My great-grandfather, William Reed, was a legend in our family. He traveled the world for some 70 years, reporting on everything from the Opium Wars in China to the discovery of King Tut's tomb. His travels became the material for grandiloquent orations at the dinner table that apparently held my grandfather and his siblings in thrall for hours.

For all his adventures, the stories my great-grandfather most liked to tell came from his experiences in a wagon train during the great westward migration on the Oregon Trail. He was just 15 at the time, but already an accomplished writer. On this, the 80th anniversary of his death, I dug through many dusty volumes of his old journals and found the remarkable pages that I enclose in this package.

William's journal is a record of anticipation and excitement, of fear and struggle for survival, of hope for a life of opportunity. He records the perils of the journey with amazing wit and immediacy. Cattle rustlers and scam artists, Indian traders and trail guides, mountain men and preachers, all come to life in these pages. To illustrate his adventure, William pasted into his journal images from the time, as well as his own drawings. He also kept a careful record of the family's finances, under the watchful eye of my great-great-grandmother.

Please consider William's journal for publication. It was his final wish that these pages should find their way into print.

Yours,

*Amanda Reed*

Amanda Reed

**EDITOR'S NOTE:**

Try as we may, we at National Geographic have not been able to locate Ms. Amanda Reed. Nor have we found a single semi-colon of William Reed's supposedly prolific writings outside of the pages of this journal. While the journal's account of life on the Oregon Trail is as accurate as any history text (and quite a lot more fun), it should be read with an attitude of skeptical inquiry. For an assessment of the facts contained in these pages, written with just such an attitude, see the afterword following Mr. Reed's journal.

# SELF-PORTRAIT
## BY WILLIAM REED

The author himself, depicted as a typical emigrant on the Oregon Trail. Taken from the pages of his journal and annotated by the 15-year-old Mr. Reed.

Pots and pans (in the hope that we will actually have something to put in them)

Blacksmith's hammer (thanks to my brother, for fixing wagon wheels and other casualties of the trail)

Flour (avoid dunking at all costs)

Extra shirt and pants, for use after the latest dunking

Sturdy boots (2,000 miles is a long way, and the wagon carries more important things; pickles for instance)

Buffalo chips, to burn for fuel

Pen and ink (significantly lighter than a hammer and in my opinion more powerful)

FLOUR

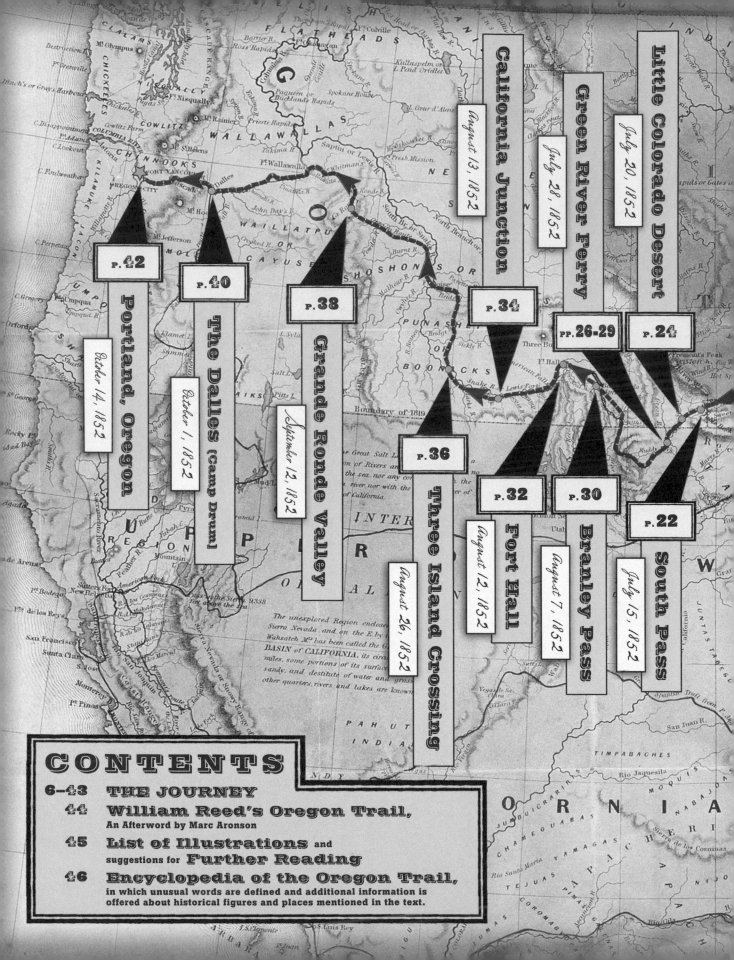

**California Junction** — *August 13, 1852* — p. 34

**Green River Ferry** — *July 28, 1852* — pp. 26-29

**Little Colorado Desert** — *July 20, 1852* — p. 24

**Portland, Oregon** — *October 14, 1852* — p. 42

**The Dalles (Camp Drum)** — *October 1, 1852* — p. 40

**Grande Ronde Valley** — *September 12, 1852* — p. 38

**Three Island Crossing** — *August 26, 1852* — p. 36

**Fort Hall** — *August 12, 1852* — p. 32

**Bradley Pass** — *August 7, 1852* — p. 30

**South Pass** — *July 15, 1852* — p. 22

# CONTENTS